T0080954

Baroque Violin Anthology 2

29 Works for Violin with Keyboard Accompaniment
29 Pièces pour Violon et accompagnement pour clavier
29 Werke für Violine mit Klavierbegleitung

Selected and edited by Walter Reiter
Sélectionnées et éditées par Walter Reiter
Ausgewählt und herausgegeben von Walter Reiter

Keyboard arrangements by Robin Bigwood
Arrangements pour clavier réalisés par Robin Bigwood
Klavierbegleitungen von Robin Bigwood

ED 13448
ISMN 979-0-2201-3298-8
ISBN 978-1-84761-272-4

www.schott-music.com

Mainz • London • Berlin • Madrid • New York • Paris • Prague • Tokyo • Toronto
© 2014 SCHOTT MUSIC Ltd, London • Printed in Germany

Acknowledgment:

Special thanks Go to Linda Reiter for help at every stage of this volume.

ED 13448
British Library Cataloguing-in-Publication Data.
A catalogue record for this book is available from the British Library
ISMN 979-0-2201-3298-8
ISBN 978-1-84761-272-4

CD recorded at Barn Cottage Studio, UK
Violin: Walter Reiter
Keyboard: Robin Bigwood
Engineer/Producer: Robin Bigwood

Cover image: Le Concert, 1630-1635, Nicolas Tournier (1590–1639). Source: The Yorck Project

French translation: Maëlys Prompsy
German translation: Heike Brühl
Music setting and page layout by Darius Heise-Krzyszton, www.notensatzstudio.de

Printed in Germany S&Co.8829

Contents / Sommaire / Inhalt

Introduction

The rich treasure house of Baroque music, fashioned by some of Western culture's greatest creative souls, overflows with material ideal for the formation of the artist of the future. The intelligent study of Baroque music opens the mind and the developing imagination to most of the major issues he or she will need to be aware of in the years to come: in a nutshell, how to make a performance of a piece of music convincing to an audience.

Sensitivity to harmony and its effects on the emotions, understanding the importance of clear musical phrases, the necessity of learning to think for oneself in a medium where the composer's written instructions are minimal, a certain freedom of rhythm and choice of dynamics, a varied and intricate use of the bow... these are just some of the benefits of studying Baroque music in detail, benefits which will continue to pay dividends when tackling music of later periods as well.

Until recently, much of this repertoire was viewed by many in the field of violin pedagogy merely as material useful enough for beginners to practise their basic techniques on, a series of somewhat simplistic stepping stones on the path to the Romantic Parnassus to which all musicians must inevitably aspire! In this book, however, each piece is considered to be a miniature masterpiece for whose convincing rendition not only artistry, but also a fair smattering of basic background knowledge is required, an approach to interpretation known today as 'historically informed' or 'historically aware'.

When exploring the music of the Baroque period, one is constantly in awe of the sheer number of composers active both in the great cities and in the tiniest of courts and churches throughout Europe. The variety of musical styles, subtly changing from town to town and from decade to decade, provides the modern performer with both challenges and rewards undreamed of a generation ago. Scholars and researchers rummaging through libraries and archives are providing us with a steady stream of works by composers sometimes not even mentioned yet in the great dictionaries of music.

This Anthology gives us the opportunity to introduce music by both known and unknown Masters and reflects, I hope, some of the excitement and joy those of us involved in the Baroque music world are privileged to feel.

In Volume Two, the right hand of the keyboard part no longer doubles the violin. The seventeenth or eighteenth-century keyboard player read from a Figured Bass line. Sometimes he could read what the other part or parts were playing, but often he just had to listen. The composer never wrote down a part for the right hand, so this had to be improvised. The player's task was thus a blend of reading, observing and contributing whatever he thought was helpful to the total sound at that particular moment.

This skill was one of many which needed to be re-learned with the revival of interest in Baroque music in the mid-twentieth century, and now constitutes an important part of the training of modern harpsichordists and organists, as well as those studying Baroque harp and lute.

The choice of accompanying instrument was sometimes specified by the composer but was often left for the performers to decide.

On the recording that Robin Bigwood and I have made for this book we used a variety of sounds, from harpsichord and organ to archlute, harp and the wonderfully invigorating squawking of the regal.

An understanding of different musical styles and the awakening of curiosity about the cultural backgrounds of the music one plays leads to an enrichment of the mind and the development of the thinking musician. To this aim, notes on every piece, written in a style accessible both to the younger and the more mature pupil have been provided, as well as a recording to help both pupil and teacher. Today, there are many resources online such as *YouTube*, where one can hear such music played by historically-informed ensembles, as well as watch the dances performed by specialists in Historic Dance.

In my extensive experience of teaching young children I have often marvelled at how easily they accept and absorb any and every musical style, from Baroque to Bartók, and how this variety stimulates them and makes their studies more interesting and enjoyable.

As a teacher of the Baroque violin to Undergraduates and Graduates in leading European Music Conservatoires, I have come to realise how much of my task in the initial stages has simply to do with helping the student think independently and intelligently about what is printed on the page of even the most basic Baroque sonata. This process of observation is the key to what many advanced violin students already in higher education seem never even to have considered, the question "what is interpretation?"

I hope that this series will make a contribution towards preparing the emerging artist to approach that key question and even, some years down the line, to begin the intelligent study of the solo music of J.S. Bach, for this generation, unlike previous ones, has come into a world in which 'historically-informed' playing constitutes an ever increasing part of the mainstream of international musical life.

Foreword

The Baroque period extends from the beginning of the 17th century, when the first violin sonatas were written in Italy, right through to around the end of the 18th century. In those almost two centuries many different styles of music came and went, constantly evolving and often differing radically from place to place, so we shouldn't really use the term 'Baroque Music' at all: 'Music in the Baroque Period' would be more accurate.

The violin we learn today, like every single instrument of the orchestra except the triangle, is very different from its 17th and 18th century ancestors. The bow, the strings and the way both violin and bow are held are also different, and so of course the sound is very different too. The notes on the page look strange to us: here is a sample of printed music from around 1640:

The whole system of writing notes, indicating rhythms and tempi, as well as rules and conventions about pitch, intonation, vibrato, rhythm, dynamics and many other aspects of playing we tend to take for granted have changed. Whereas nowadays we are taught to play the notes exactly as they are written, our Baroque counterparts would have regarded the text as a mere framework around which they were free to improvise.

Much of the theory of music which is taught today, as well as certain aspects of violin technique, are not applicable to the Baroque repertoire. Therefore, in order to play Baroque music the way the composers intended it to be played, and thus to do it full justice, we need to have some guidance. Just as we cannot play Japanese or Arabic music without first learning something about them, we cannot play the music of the now vanished Baroque civilization as if it had all been written yesterday! We need some background knowledge. Luckily for us, there are many texts from the period telling us about how to play the instrument and also how to play the music. This book uses that knowledge, and provides the emerging violinist with a first exploration into the Baroque repertoire.

Johann Sebastian Bach (1685-1750)

Many pieces in this book are either dances or have a clear dance element woven into their fabric. Such pieces should sound like dances, with all the rhythmic interest, stresses and articulations clearly stated. This necessitates the nurturing of a more lively bow technique, of a bowing arm which dances, often leaving the string. Vibrato in dances is not advisable. It slows the bow down and stops it dancing: save it for the more lyrical passages! I have bowed each piece according to both stylistic and musical criterion. Essential to a true interpretation of Baroque music is the hierarchy of strong and weak beats. Important notes should be stressed and less important ones made to sound weaker, thus achieving a kind of sonorous perspective.

Walter Reiter (2014)

Introduction

L'étude approfondie de la musique de la période baroque permet à l'élève de développer son imagination et d'ouvrir son esprit, encore jeune, aux réalités du monde, qu'il ou elle aura besoin de connaître dans les années à venir : en un mot, apprendre à rendre convaincant un morceau de musique pour un public.

Voici quelques avantages que l'on acquiert en étudiant la musique baroque : être sensible à l'harmonie et à ses effets sur les émotions, saisir l'importance de phrases musicales claires, apprendre à penser pour soi, avoir une certaine liberté dans le rythme et le choix des nuances, utiliser de façon variée et complexe l'archet. Tout ceci sera très bénéfique pour l'étude de musique de périodes ultérieures.

Il y a encore peu de temps, la majeure partie de ce répertoire était simplement considérée comme un outil pédagogique utile pour les débutants qui souhaitaient améliorer leurs techniques de base. Dans ce livre en revanche, chaque morceau est considéré tel un chef d'œuvre miniature pour lequel non seulement une interprétation convaincante et artistique est requise, mais de réelles notions de base d'interprétation sont également apportées ; une approche qui se veut « conforme à la musique de l'époque ».

Lorsque l'on se penche sur la musique de la période baroque, on est toujours étonné du nombre impressionnant de compositeurs alors actifs dans toute l'Europe à la fois dans les grandes villes et dans les Cours et églises les plus petites. Grâce à la variété de styles musicaux, changeant légèrement en fonction des villes et des décennies, l'interprète moderne est face à des challenges et des récompenses, non imaginés par une génération précédente. Spécialistes et chercheurs parcourant bibliothèques et archives nous fournissent un apport régulier d'œuvres de compositeurs, qui ne sont souvent même pas encore cités dans les grands dictionnaires de musique.

Grâce à cette anthologie, nous pouvons proposer des œuvres de maîtres plus ou moins connus et ainsi ressentir, je l'espère, un peu de cet enthousiasme et cette joie qui font le privilège de ceux concernés par l'univers de la musique baroque.

Dans ce deuxième volume, la partie de main droite du clavier ne double plus celle du violon. Le claviériste du dix-septième ou dix-huitième siècle improvisait sur une basse figurée. Parfois il pouvait aussi lire une ou plusieurs parties des autres instruments, mais le plus souvent, il devait simplement écouter. Le compositeur n'écrivait jamais de partie pour la main droite, qui devait donc être improvisée. L'interprète devait donc mêler lecture, observation et jeu aux moments qu'il jugeait opportuns en fonction du rendu de la musique dans son ensemble.

Au milieu du vingtième siècle, avec le regain d'intérêt pour la musique baroque, cette compétence devait donc être réapprise, entre autres. Elle constitue désormais une part importante de la formation des clavecinistes et organistes modernes, mais aussi de ceux apprenant la harpe et le luth baroques. Le compositeur spécifiait parfois le choix de l'instrument d'accompagnement, mais souvent c'était les interprètes qui décidaient. Sur l'enregistrement que j'ai réalisé avec Robin Bigwood, nous avons utilisé plusieurs instrumentations, du clavecin à l'orgue en passant par l'archiluth, la harpe et le son merveilleux et tonifiant du régal.

De plus, vous trouverez des notes sur chacun des morceaux, écrites dans un style accessible aux élèves plus ou moins avancés, et des enregistrements, pour aider l'élève et le professeur. De nos jours, il existe de multiples ressources en ligne, comme *YouTube*, grâce auxquelles on peut écouter des ensembles jouer selon cette approche historique, et regarder des danseurs spécialistes des danses baroques.

Grâce à ma longue expérience de professeur pour jeunes enfants, je reste souvent émerveillé de voir qu'ils assimilent facilement tout style de musique, du Baroque à Bartók, et que cette variété rend leur apprentissage plus intéressant et agréable.

En tant que professeur de violon baroque dans différents cycles des plus grands conservatoires de musique européens, la plus grande partie de mon travail consiste à aider l'élève, au début de son apprentissage, à penser par lui même et à avoir un regard intelligent sur la partition, même lorsqu'il s'agit des sonates baroques les plus simples. Ce temps d'observation est la clé de la réponse à la question « qu'est ce que l'interprétation ? », à laquelle bon nombre de violonistes expérimentés ne semblent avoir jamais réfléchi.

J'espère qu'avec ces recueils tout jeune artiste se penchera sur cette question clé, dans un monde où cette approche historique constitue une part toujours croissante dans la musique internationale.

Préface

La période baroque s'étend du début du XVIIè siècle, quand apparaissent en Italie les premières sonates pour violons, jusqu'en 1750 environ. Au fil de ces 150 ans, de nombreux styles de musique émergent, plus ou moins éphémères, en constante évolution et différant radicalement en fonction des régions. C'est pourquoi nous ne devrions pas utiliser l'expression « musique baroque » mais plutôt celle plus appropriée de « musique de la période baroque ». Le violon tel qu'il est enseigné aujourd'hui, et comme chacun des instruments de l'orchestre, est loin de ses ancêtres des XVIIè et XVIIIè siècles. L'archet, les cordes et la façon de tenir le violon et l'archet diffèrent, et donc bien sûr le son. Les notes de la partition ne nous sont pas familières. Voici un exemple de musique imprimée vers 1640:

Tout le système d'écriture des notes, d'indications de rythme, de tempi, des règles et conventions sur le ton, les intonations, les vibratos, les rythmiques et nuances et bien d'autres indications de jeu que nous avons tendance à prendre pour acquis, a évolué.

Alors que de nos jours on nous apprend à jouer uniquement les notes telles qu'elles sont écrites sur la partition, à l'époque baroque, cette dernière est considérée comme une simple structure, qui laisse libre cours à l'improvisation.

Une grande partie de la théorie musicale enseignée aujourd'hui ainsi que certaines techniques propres au violon ne peuvent être réellement appliquées au répertoire baroque. C'est pourquoi, afin de pouvoir jouer la musique baroque comme elle fut pensée par ses compositeurs, nous avons besoin de conseils. Heureusement pour nous, de nombreux textes de cette époque nous expliquent la manière de jouer du violon et d'interpréter la musique. Ce livre s'en inspire et apporte au jeune violoniste un premier aperçu du répertoire baroque.

Johann Sebastian Bach (1685-1750)

Dans ce recueil, de nombreuses pièces sont soit des danses, soit s'en rapprochent subtilement. De telles pièces doivent donc laisser transparaître cet effet de danse par le rythme, les accents et les articulations clairement exprimés. Il faut donc approfondir une technique de tenue d'archet plus entraînante, où le bras danse et souvent s'éloigne de la corde. Pour les danses, il est déconseillé de faire des vibratos. Ils ralentissent l'archet et cassent l'effet dansant : gardez les vibratos pour les passages plus lyriques ! Sur chaque morceau, j'ai indiqué les coups d'archet en accord avec le style et la musique. Pour interpréter correctement la musique baroque, il est primordial de savoir distinguer les temps forts des temps faibles. Les notes importantes doivent être accentuées, les autres sont plus légères, donnant ainsi de la perspective à la musique.

Walter Reiter (2014)

Einleitung

Eine Auseinandersetzung mit der Barockmusik öffnet Geist und
Fantasie der jungen Schüler für die meisten wichtigen Aspekte, die
sie in den kommenden Jahren beachten müssen: Kurz gesagt, wie
ein Stück gespielt werden muss, um das Publikum zu überzeugen.
Einen Sinn für Harmonien und ihre emotionale Wirkung zu entwickeln, die Bedeutung klarer musikalischer Phrasen zu verstehen,
eigenständig denken zu lernen, eine gewisse rhythmische und
dynamische Freiheit sowie eine abwechslungsreiche und versierte
Bogenführung zu entwickeln... dies sind nur einige Vorteile, die
aus der Auseinandersetzung mit der Barockmusik entstehen und
sich bei der Beschäftigung mit der Musik späterer Epochen bezahlt
machen.

Bis vor kurzem galten die meisten Spielstücke häufig als lediglich
für Anfänger geeignet, die damit Grundtechniken üben konnten.
In diesem Buch wird jedoch jedes Stück als kleines Meisterwerk
betrachtet, für dessen überzeugende Interpretation nicht nur
Kunstfertigkeit erforderlich ist, sondern auch einige Grundkennt-
nisse über den Hintergrund der Stücke – ein Interpretationsan-
satz, der heute als „geschichtskundig" bzw. „geschichtsbewusst"
bezeichnet wird.

Wenn man sich mit der Barockzeit befasst, ist man immer wieder
erstaunt, wie viele Komponisten sowohl in den großen Städten als
auch an den kleinsten Höfen und Kirchen in ganz Europa tätig
waren. In den vielen musikalischen Stilrichtungen, die sich von
Stadt zu Stadt und von Jahrzehnt zu Jahrzehnt leicht veränderten,
finden heutige Interpreten sowohl Herausforderungen als auch
Schätze, die vor einer Generation noch völlig unbekannt waren.
Wissenschaftler und Forscher zaubern aus ihren Bibliotheken und
Archiven permanent Werke von Komponisten für uns hervor,
die teilweise noch gar nicht in den großen Musiklexika erwähnt
werden.

Die vorliegende Anthologie bietet die Gelegenheit, Musik von
bekannten und unbekannten Meistern vorzustellen und spiegelt,
so hoffe ich, die Begeisterung wider, die wir Musikwissenschaftler
bei der Erforschung der Barockmusik empfinden.

In Band 2 spielt die rechte Hand am Klavier nicht mehr dasselbe
wie die Violine. Der Klavierspieler des 17. bzw. 18. Jahrhunderts
orientierte sich an einer Generalbassstimme. Manchmal konnte er
mitlesen, was die anderen Stimmen spielten, oft musste er jedoch
einfach zuhören. Eine Stimme für die rechte Hand wurde nicht
notiert, so dass sie improvisiert werden musste. Der Interpret hatte
folglich die Aufgabe, mitzulesen, zu beobachten und dann das
beizusteuern, was er im jeweiligen Moment als Bereicherung des
Gesamtklangs empfand.

Diese Fähigkeit war eine von vielen, die mit dem wieder auflebenn-
den Interesse an der Barockmusik Mitte des 20. Jahrhunderts neu
erlernt werden musste. Heute ist sie ein wichtiger Bestandteil der
Ausbildung von Cembalisten und Organisten sowie des Studiums
der Barockharfe und Laute.

Das Begleitinstrument wurde zwar manchmal vom Komponisten
vorgegeben, doch oblag die Wahl meist den Interpreten. Die Aufnahmen, die Robin Bigwood und ich für dieses Buch eingespielt
haben, enthalten verschiedene Instrumente, von Cembalo und
Orgel bis zur Erzlaute, Harfe und dem herrlich erfrischenden
Gequäke des Regals.

Das Buch enthält zu jedem Stück Anmerkungen, die so geschrieben
sind, dass sie sowohl junge als auch etwas ältere Schüler anspre-
chen. Außerdem ist eine CD zur Unterstützung von Schülern
und Lehrern enthalten. Heute gibt es viele Quellen im Internet,
z.B. *YouTube*, wo solche Musik von geschichtskundigen Ensembles
gespielt wird und man sich Tänze anschauen kann, die von Spezi-
alisten historischer Tänze gezeigt werden.

In meiner langjährigen Erfahrung mit jungen Schülern war ich
immer wieder erstaunt, wie leicht sie jeden Musikstil von Barock
bis Bartók in sich aufnehmen, und wie sehr diese Vielfalt ihr Üben
bereichert. Als Lehrer, der Studierende führender europäischer
Konservatorien im Fach Barockvioline unterrichtet, besteht
meine Aufgabe zunächst darin, den Studierenden zu helfen,
unvoreingenommen und rational über die abgedruckten Noten
nachzudenken, und sei die Barocksonate, zu der sie gehören, auch
noch so einfach.

Dieser Beobachtungsprozess ist der Schlüssel zu der Frage, die viele
fortgeschrittene Geigenschüler anscheinend noch nie berücksichtigt
haben: „Was ist Interpretation?"

Ich hoffe, dass diese Reihe einen Beitrag zu einer besseren Vorbe-
reitung angehender Künstler auf diese Frage leistet – in einer Welt,
in der das „geschichtskundige" Spielen eines Instruments im Mainstream der internationalen Musikszene immer weiter zunimmt.

Vorwort

Die Barockzeit begann Anfang des 17. Jahrhunderts, als in Italien
die ersten Violinsonaten geschrieben wurden, und endete um
1750. In diesen 150 Jahren kamen und gingen viele verschiedene
Musikrichtungen – ständig entstanden neue, die oft regional sehr
unterschiedlich waren. Daher sollte man den Begriff „Barockmusik" eigentlich gar nicht verwenden. „Musik der Barockzeit"
würde es besser treffen.

Die Violine, die heute gespielt wird, unterscheidet sich wie jedes
andere Instrument deutlich von ihren Vorfahren aus dem 17. und
18. Jahrhundert. Bogen, Saiten und die Art und Weise, wie Violine
und Bogen gehalten werden, sind anders, und auch der Klang hat
sich stark verändert.

Heute wird den Schülern beigebracht, die Noten exakt so zu spielen, wie sie notiert sind. Die Barockviolinisten hingegen betrach-
teten die Noten lediglich als Rahmen, in dem sie nach Belieben
improvisieren konnten.

Das gesamte Notationssystem einschließlich Rhythmik und Tempi, die Normen und Konventionen bezüglich Tonlage, Intonation, Vibrato, Rhythmus, Dynamik und viele andere spielerische Aspekte, die für uns selbstverständlich sind, haben sich verändert.

Ein Großteil der heute gelehrten Musiktheorie sowie bestimmte technische Aspekte des Geigenspiels können nicht auf das Barockrepertoire angewandt werden. Daher brauchen wir eine Anleitung, wenn wir Barockmusik so spielen wollen, wie es vom Komponisten beabsichtigt wurde. Glücklicherweise gibt es viele Texte aus der Barockzeit mit Hinweisen, wie das Instrument und die Musik gespielt werden sollen. Dieses Buch baut auf diesem Wissen auf und bietet jungen Geigern eine erste Orientierungshilfe für barocke Spielstücke.

Johann Sebastian Bach (1685-1750)

Viele Stücke in diesem Buch sind Tänze oder weisen deutliche Merkmale eines Tanzes auf. Solche Stücke sollten auch wie Tänze klingen – mit allen rhythmischen Belangen, Betonungen und angegebenen Artikulationsarten. Dies erfordert eine lebhaftere Bogentechnik, einen Arm, der „tanzt" und häufig die Saite verlässt. Vibrato ist in Tänzen nicht angebracht. Es verlangsamt den Bogen und verhindert, dass er tanzt. Daher sollte man es sich für gefühlvollere Passagen aufheben. Ich habe die Bogenführung in jedem Stück den stilistischen und musikalischen Kriterien angepasst. Wichtig für eine authentische Interpretation der Barockmusik ist die Hierarchie aus starken und schwachen Zählzeiten. Wichtige Noten sollten betont und weniger wichtige schwächer gespielt werden. Somit entsteht eine Art Klangperspektive.

Walter Reiter (2014)

Three Jacobean Masque Tunes

1. The Mountebank's Dance at Grayes Inn

Anonymous
Ed. Walter Reiter, arr. Robin Bigwood

D. C. senza repetizione
al Fine

2. Adsonns Maske

John Adson (c. 1587–1640)
Ed. Walter Reiter, arr. Robin Bigwood

Not too fast

3. Sir Francis Bacon's Second Masque

Anonymous
Ed. Walter Reiter, arr. Robin Bigwood

Three songs from 'Le nuove musiche'

4. Dalla porta d'oriente

Giulio Caccini (1551–1618)
Ed. Walter Reiter, arr. Robin Bigwood

5. Al fonte, al prato

Giulio Caccini (1551–1618)
Ed. Walter Reiter, arr. Robin Bigwood

[Ritornello]

6. Amor, ch'attendi

Giulio Caccini (1551–1618)
Ed. Walter Reiter, arr. Robin Bigwood

7. Symphonia Septima 'La Gianina'

from *Sinfonie boscarecia*, Op. 8

Marco Uccellini (c.1603–1680)
Ed. Walter Reiter, arr. Robin Bigwood

8. Symphonia Decima Settima 'La Stucgarda'
from *Sinfonie Boscarecia*, Op. 8

Marco Uccellini (c.1603–1680)
Ed. Walter Reiter, arr. Robin Bigwood

9. Sonata Seconda

Tomaso Cecchino (1583–1644)
Ed. Walter Reiter, arr. Robin Bigwood

10. Menuet BWV Anh. 132

from *The Notebook of Anna Magdalena Bach* (1725)

J. S. Bach (1685–1750)
Ed. Walter Reiter, arr. Robin Bigwood

11. Bist du bei mir BWV 508

from *The Notebook of Anna Magdalena Bach* (1725)

Gottfrid Heinrich Stölzel (1690–1749)
Ed. Walter Reiter, arr. Robin Bigwood

Fine

D. S. al Fine

12. Musette
from *The Notebook of Anna Magdalena Bach* (1725)

J. S. Bach (1685–1750)
Ed. Walter Reiter, arr. Robin Bigwood

Fine

D. C. senza repetizione al Fine

13. Menuet BWV Anh. 115
from *The Notebook of Anna Magdalena Bach* (1725)

Christian Petzold (1677–1733)
Ed. Walter Reiter, arr. Robin Bigwood

14. Polonaise BWV Anh. 119

from *The Notebook of Anna Magdalena Bach* (1725)

J. S. Bach (1685–1750)
Ed. Walter Reiter, arr. Robin Bigwood

15. Allegro
from *Sonata VII*

William Babell (c.1690–1723)
Ed. Walter Reiter, arr. Robin Bigwood

Fine

D. C. al Fine

16. La Villageoise
from *Pièces de clavecin* (1724)

Jean-Philippe Rameau (1683–1764)
Ed. Walter Reiter, arr. Robin Bigwood

17. Gavotta

Martino Bitti (1655–1743)
Ed. Walter Reiter, arr. Robin Bigwood

18. Greensleeves

Anonymous, Old English Melody
Ed. Walter Reiter, arr. Robin Bigwood

■ Violin

Baroque Violin Anthology 2

29 Works for Violin with Keyboard Accompaniment selected and edited by Walter Reiter
29 Pièces pour Violon et accompagnement pour clavier sélectionnées et éditées par Walter Reiter
29 Werke für Violine mit Klavierbegleitung ausgewählt und herausgegeben von Walter Reiter

Contents / Sommaire / Inhalt

ED 13448
ISMN 979-0-2201-3298-8
ISBN 978-1-84761-272-4

Mainz • London • Berlin • Madrid • New York • Paris • Prague • Tokyo • Toronto
© 2014 SCHOTT MUSIC Ltd, London • Printed in Germany

Three Jacobean Masque Tunes

1. The Mountebank's Dance at Grayes Inn

Anonymous
Ed. Walter Reiter, arr. Robin Bigwood

2. Adsonns Maske

John Adson (c. 1587–1640)
Ed. Walter Reiter, arr. Robin Bigwood

3. Sir Francis Bacon's Second Masque

Anonymous
Ed. Walter Reiter, arr. Robin Bigwood

Three songs from 'Le nuove musiche'

4. Dalla porta d'oriente

Giulio Caccini (1551–1618)
Ed. Walter Reiter, arr. Robin Bigwood

5. Al fonte, al prato

Giulio Caccini (1551–1618)
Ed. Walter Reiter, arr. Robin Bigwood

6. Amor, ch'attendi

Giulio Caccini (1551–1618)
Ed. Walter Reiter, arr. Robin Bigwood

7. Symphonia Septima 'La Gianina'

from *Sinfonie boscarecia,* Op. 8

Marco Uccellini (c.1603–1680)
Ed. Walter Reiter, arr. Robin Bigwood

8. Symphonia Decima Settima 'La Stucgarda'

from *Sinfonie Boscarecia*, Op. 8

Marco Uccellini (c.1603–1680)
Ed. Walter Reiter, arr. Robin Bigwood

9. Sonata Seconda

Tomaso Cecchino (1583–1644)
Ed. Walter Reiter, arr. Robin Bigwood

10. Menuet BWV Anh. 132

from *The Notebook of Anna Magdalena Bach* (1725)

J. S. Bach (1685–1750)
Ed. Walter Reiter, arr. Robin Bigwood

11. Bist du bei mir BWV 508

from *The Notebook of Anna Magdalena Bach* (1725)

Gottfrid Heinrich Stölzel (1690–1749)
Ed. Walter Reiter, arr. Robin Bigwood

Fine

13. Menuet BWV Anh. 115

from *The Notebook of Anna Magdalena Bach* (1725)

Christian Petzold (1677–1733)
Ed. Walter Reiter, arr. Robin Bigwood

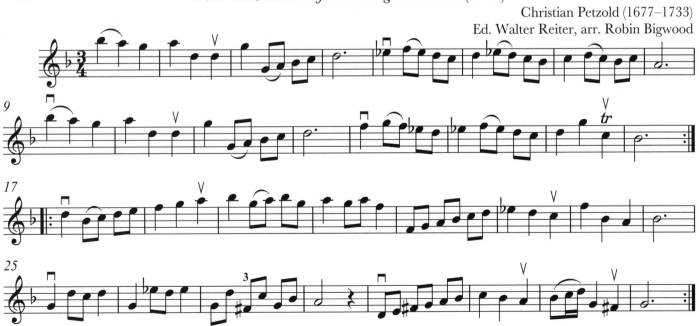

14. Polonaise BWV Anh. 119
from *The Notebook of Anna Magdalena Bach* (1725)

J. S. Bach (1685–1750)
Ed. Walter Reiter, arr. Robin Bigwood

15. Allegro
from *Sonata VII*

William Babell (c.1690–1723)
Ed. Walter Reiter, arr. Robin Bigwood

Fine

D. C. al Fine

16. La Villageoise

from *Pièces de clavecin* (1724)

Jean-Philippe Rameau (1683–1764)
Ed. Walter Reiter, arr. Robin Bigwood

17. Gavotta

Martino Bitti (1655–1743)
Ed. Walter Reiter, arr. Robin Bigwood

18. Greensleeves

Anonymous, Old English Melody
Ed. Walter Reiter, arr. Robin Bigwood

19. Adagio
from *Sonata in D* RV 798

Antonio Vivaldi (1678–1741)
Ed. Walter Reiter, arr. Robin Bigwood

20. Allegro
from *Sonata in D* RV 798

Antonio Vivaldi (1678–1741)
Ed. Walter Reiter, arr. Robin Bigwood

21. Rondeau

from *Abdelazar*

Henry Purcell (1659–1695)
Ed. Walter Reiter, arr. Robin Bigwood

22. Sonata Terza

Giovanni Battista Fontana (1589?–1630)
Ed. Walter Reiter, arr. Robin Bigwood

23. Preludio
from *Sonata No. 10*

Arcangelo Corelli (1653–1713)
Ed. Walter Reiter, arr. Robin Bigwood

16

24. Ballo

Giovanni Battista degli Antonii (1636–1698)
Ed. Walter Reiter, arr. Robin Bigwood

25. Ballo

Giovanni Battista degli Antonii (1636–1698)
Ed. Walter Reiter, arr. Robin Bigwood

26. Andante
from *Sonata No. 5*

George Frederic Handel (1685–1759)
Ed. Walter Reiter, arr. Robin Bigwood

17

27. Boure
from *Sonata No. 5*

George Frederic Handel (1685–1759)
Ed. Walter Reiter, arr. Robin Bigwood

© 2014 Schott Music Ltd, London

28. Sarabanda
from *Sonata No. 7*

Arcangelo Corelli (1653–1713)
Ed. Walter Reiter, arr. Robin Bigwood

Largo

© 2014 Schott Music Ltd, London

29. A Division on a Ground

Michel Farinel (1649-1726)
Ed. Walter Reiter, arr. Robin Bigwood

19. Adagio
from *Sonata in D* RV 798

Antonio Vivaldi (1678–1741)
Ed. Walter Reiter, arr. Robin Bigwood

20. Allegro
from *Sonata in D* RV 798

Antonio Vivaldi (1678–1741)
Ed. Walter Reiter, arr. Robin Bigwood

21. Rondeau
from *Abdelazar*

Henry Purcell (1659–1695)
Ed. Walter Reiter, arr. Robin Bigwood

22. Sonata Terza

Giovanni Battista Fontana (1589?–1630)
Ed. Walter Reiter, arr. Robin Bigwood

23. Preludio

from *Sonata No. 10*

Arcangelo Corelli (1653–1713)
Ed. Walter Reiter, arr. Robin Bigwood

Adagio

24. Ballo

Giovanni Battista degli Antonii (1636–1698)
Ed. Walter Reiter, arr. Robin Bigwood

25. Ballo

Giovanni Battista degli Antonii (1636–1698)
Ed. Walter Reiter, arr. Robin Bigwood

26. Andante

from *Sonata No. 5*

George Frederic Handel (1685–1759)
Ed. Walter Reiter, arr. Robin Bigwood

27. Boure
from *Sonata No. 5*

George Frederic Handel (1685–1759)
Ed. Walter Reiter, arr. Robin Bigwood

28. Sarabanda
from *Sonata No. 7*

Arcangelo Corelli (1653–1713)
Ed. Walter Reiter, arr. Robin Bigwood

Largo

29. A Division on a Ground

Michel Farinel (1649-1726)
Ed. Walter Reiter, arr. Robin Bigwood

Notes on the Pieces and the Composers

Three Jacobean Masque Tunes

1. The Mountebank's Dance at Grayes Inne

2. Adsonns Maske

3. Sir Francis Bacon's Second Masque

The word 'Jacobean' is derived from Jacobus, the Latin form of the English name James, and refers to the reign of King James VI of Scotland, who was crowned King James I of England in 1603. A masque was an extravagant entertainment, usually performed for kings and queens, with music, dancing, singing and acting performed by masquers in glamorous costumes and with wonderful stage scenery in the background.

• The first and third pieces mostly have the character of dances: play them with a vigorous bow, in such a way that your audience will really want to dance!

The Mountebank's Masque was produced in 1618 at Gray's Inn in London (a mountebank is a swindler!)

• The fast section should be played at twice the speed of the more graceful opening slow section.

John Adson (1587–1640) was an English composer and musician, who worked mostly in theatres. His 'Maske' has a more lyrical quality than the other two.

Francis Bacon (1561–1626) was a very influential man of many talents: philosopher, scientist, statesman, and author. This tune, written in his honour, has a stately dignity to it, although the last section sounds more like a folk dance!

Giulio Caccini (1551–1618)

Three songs from 'Le nuove musiche'

4. Dalla porta d'oriente

5. Al fonte, al prato

6. Amor, chlattendi

Giulio Caccini was an Italian singer and composer who also played the harp and the lute. In his collection of solo songs *Le nuove musiche* (*The New Music*, 1602) the vocal line expressed as closely as possible the meaning of the words, helped by the harmony of the Bass Continuo. This changed the course of musical history and made possible the birth of opera and of the solo sonata.

• The three pieces included here are all songs, and we have marked the breaths a singer would take with commas. You too should breathe at the commas, both physically and by lifting your bow slightly above the string. Every book about instrumental music from the sixteenth century onwards talks about how we must imitate singers: why not find recordings of these songs and imitate them!

Marco Uccellini (c.1603–1680)

From Sinfonie Boscarecia, op. 8

7. Symphonia Septima 'La Gianina'

8. Symphonia Decima Settima 'La Stucgarda'

Marco Uccellini was an Italian composer and violinist. He worked in Modena and later became 'maestro di cappella' (music director) of a church in Parma. He wrote operas and ballets, which have sadly all been lost, as well as many sonatas (some of which go as high as the 6th position). These 'Symphoniae' (not 'Symphonies

in the later, classical sense) meaning an instrumental piece, all have names, because each was dedicated to a different lady!

• Listen carefully to the recording and observe how the sound varies from section to section. A section in a minor key is often gentler than one that is major.

Tomaso Cecchino (1583–1644)

9. Sonata Secondo

Venice is a uniquely beautiful city, with its canals, splendid palaces and magnificent churches. In former times, it was the capital of a country, the Venetian Republic. Tomaso Cecchino worked much of his life in a part of that country which today is in Croatia. Like most early 17th-century sonatas, this piece would have been performed on any instrument capable of playing the notes: a recorder, a *cornetto* (a kind of wooden trumpet) or a violin.

• Notice that the bass, which opens the movement, is entirely equal in importance to the top part. If you have a friend who plays the cello or the bassoon, you could play this piece as a duet. It is important to make the phrases clear: the bowings I have added will help achieve this.

From 'The Notebook of Anna Magdelaena Bach' (1725)
J.S. Bach (1685–1750)

10. Menuet (BWV Anh. 132)

Play this with a singing tone, never forgetting the elegance and poise which are essential to the correct execution of any Minuet.

• In bar 2 and similar places, allow your bow to dance lightly, shortening the notes a small amount, allowing a little light into the sound.

From 'The Notebook of Anna Magdelaena Bach' (1725)
Gottfried Heinrich Stölzel (1690–1749)

11. Bist du bei mir (BWV Anh. 119)

Bist du bei mir ('Art thou with me?') is a beautiful song which was long thought to be by Bach, but is now known to be from an opera by Gottfried Heinrich Stölzel.

• Your bow is your voice: it must sing! The more expressive the gestures you make with your bow-arm, the more expressive your sound will be.

• In bar 13 the trill begins with an expressive appoggiatura and should not be too fast (being a fourth finger trill, this should be easy to do!)

From 'The Notebook of Anna Magdelaena Bach' (1725)
J.S. Bach (1685–1750)

12. Musette

A 'musette' is a dance named after a French Bagpipe. Although there is no drone in this one, the Bass part does repeat the same note in a similar way.

• In bars 3 and 4 shorten the quavers, contrasting with the more singing character of the first two bars.

• Bars 13 and 14 should be played gently and lyrically. The syncopated notes should be gentle too, not heavy.

48

From 'The Notebook of Anna Magdelaena Bach' (1725)
Christian Petzold (1677–1733)
13. Menuet (BWV Anh. 115)

Like No. 10, this minuet is in a minor key. It was written by Christian Petzold a German composer and organist. The first four notes must be sung, but the next two can be 'neglected' (they are less important). Learning to distinguish between important and less important notes (they were called 'good' and 'bad' in Bach's time) is essential if this music is not to become dull.

From 'The Notebook of Anna Magdelaena Bach' (1725)
J.S. Bach (1685–1750)
14. Polonaise (BWV Anh. 119)

A 'polonaise' is a Polish dance, not too fast, but very rhythmic and of noble character. Many Baroque composers used it in their compositions, and it remained popular well into the 19th century.
• Use short, crisp bows for this piece. The beginning of each bar has a healthy accent!

William Babell (c.1690–1723)
15. Allegro from Sonata VII

William Babell was an English harpsichordist, organist, violinist and composer, who had possibly studied with Handel. Improvisation (the art of playing music which is not written down, rather like Jazz musicians do today) was an essential part of a Baroque musician's skill, and Babell was especially famous for being able to take a melody and improvise his own version of it on the spot: some people thought that he was a better improviser than even Handel himself!
• Improvising dynamics was one aspect of this skill. Composers rarely wrote dynamic markings in the Baroque period, but playing with no dynamics would make the music dreadfully dull! I haven't added any to your part, so you're going to have to make them up! As a first step, try this simple device: notes that go upwards are played *crescendo* and notes that descend are played *diminuendo*. In other words, the dynamics follow the line that you see on the page. By using different amounts of bow for each note, you will easily achieve this.

Jean-Philippe Rameau (1683–1764)
16. La Villageoise

Jean-Philippe Rameau was one of France's greatest harpsichordists, theorists and composers. He was a self-taught musician who wrote many important books on harmony. Amazingly, he wrote his first opera at the age of 50 and went on to write 20 more in his long life. *La Villageoise* ("The Village Girl") comes from his Suite in E minor for harpsichord. See if you can find a recording online played on the harpsichord: how different it sounds from a recording on the piano, conjuring up visions of an age of elegance and sophistication!
• As this music has something of a dance-like character, make sure you don't play it as if it were a song: the notes should often be a little shorter than their theoretical value. The first bar is a good example of this.
• Moreover, not all notes of the same value are equal: the second notes of bars 1, 2 and 4, for example, are weak, bouncing off the stronger first beats. The syncopated notes in bars 18, 20 and 22, on the other hand, need a stronger but graceful gesture of the bow. The down-bows I have added will help achieve this and will shorten the first, weaker notes of those bars. You will soon learn to recognise the difference between strong beats and weak beats, helping to make the music both elegant and interesting.

Martino Bitti (1655–1743)
17. Gavotta

Martino Bitti was an Italian violinist and composer, working mainly in Florence.
The Gavotte was originally a French folk dance, and was popular throughout the Baroque era. It begins on the last beat of the bar.
• Bars 2, 4 and 6 are strong, but bars 1, 3 and 5 are weak. If you accent the first beat of a weak bar, it will destroy the balance of the music!

Old English Melody
18. Greensleeves

Greensleeves is an old English melody. First mentioned in 1580 and referred to in The Merry Wives of *Windsor* by Shakespeare, it has remained a popular tune ever since. This version, which is probably different from the one you know, comes from a collection called *The Division Violin*, first published in 1685 by John Playford, a London bookseller.
• Each 8-bar section is a variation on the theme, written over a repeated Bass. Some of the bowings are quite tricky: make sure you make the bow dance!
• Once you've mastered the piece, you can add your own variations: just get a friend to repeat the bass line over and over, while you play whatever comes into your head… providing it more or less fits! It's certainly fun to try, and don't be put off if you go wrong! You'll make many mistakes at first, but eventually you'll get the hang of it. Improvising divisions and ornaments was part of every musician's training until well into the 19th-century, and it still is with Jazz musicians and in most non-Western musical traditions. Let's make it part of our education too!

Antonio Vivaldi (1678–1741)
*19. Adagio from Sonata in D (*RV 798)

Antonio Vivaldi was an Italian violinist and composer. For eleven years he was 'maestro di violino' at the Ospedale della Pietà in his native Venice, teaching the violin to young ladies and writing works especially for them. Today, Vivaldi is best known for The *Four Seasons*, but in all he wrote 500 concertos, much church music and many operas.
• The Adagio (the word means 'at ease') should not be played too slowly: the quaver bass line suggests a constant forwards motion. Be careful not to accent the quaver up-bows, such as the ones in bars 1, 2 and 3: you will need to lighten them, compensating for the increase in speed.
• On the recording you can hear both the written version and a version I have ornamented in the way Vivaldi himself might have done. How do I know? Because there are many books written throughout the Baroque period on how to ornament. Once you know the piece well, you can try your hand at making up your own!

20. Allegro from Sonata in D (RV 798)

In the Allegro, keep the bow lively and light throughout. Remember to vary the dynamics by following the contour of the notes: up is crescendo and down is diminuendo.
• If we play notes too equally, it can make the music very heavy. The fact is, some notes are more important than others! In Bars 1 and 2, and in similar places, give a good impulse to the first note and allow the next two notes to bounce passively off it, as if your bow were a bouncing ball. The last note of each bar is then re-

energised, giving the bar the same rhythm as the Bass.

• Likewise Bar 8 and similar should have a single, active impulse on the first note, the next four notes being a passive reaction to that impulse. Bar 23, and others similar to it, should also have a single impulse on the first note: don't work the bow too hard for the rest of the bar, as that will make it sound heavy, as if there are 'too many' notes.

Henry Purcell (1659–1695)

21. *Rondeau* from *Abdelazar*

Henry Purcell is arguably the greatest of all English composers. In his very short life he composed music for the church, the theatre and the court, as well as much vocal and chamber music. He is remarkable for the wide range of emotions he is capable of making us feel, his music sometimes uplifting and even funny, sometimes almost unbearably sad. Purcell wrote this music for a 1695 production of the play *Abdelazar*, or "The Moor's Revenge", by Aphra Behn, one of the earliest female authors. The *Rondo* became famous when Benjamin Britten used it as the theme for his *Young Person's Guide to the Orchestra* some 250 years later.

A rondo (Purcell spells it the French way, "Rondeau") is a composition in which an opening theme (the first 8 bars) reappears several times (at bars 9, 17 and 33) while in between, there are contrasting sections called 'episodes.'

• Play the theme in a boisterous, majestic manner, with crisp bow strokes. The rhythm in bars 3-6 follows the bass, with an accented first and last note of each bar. The episode that begins in bar 25 is the gentlest, most lyrical section.

The Sonata was 'invented' in Italy, but many Italian composers worked abroad, in countries as far apart as England and Poland, taking with them the new baroque styles and techniques.

Giovanni Battista Fontana (1589(?)–1630)

22. *Sonata Terza*

Giovanni Battista Fontana was an Italian violinist and composer, about whose life we know very little. His six sonatas for solo violin and continuo form part of a collection of sonatas for one, two and three violins published in 1641. These works are among the most important examples of the early solo sonata.

One feature of these early 17th century sonatas is that they had no 'movements' in the later sense, but were divided into many contrasting sections linked together.

Sonata Terza (Sonata No. 3) has many sections, but I've left some out to make it shorter and simpler: if you want to listen to the whole work you can certainly find recordings online, played on violins or other instruments.

• We have seen the rhythm in the opening bar before: it was a common rhythm in Venetian music, and has a fanfare-like quality. Mostly though, the first section can be played quite lyrically, with a singing bow.

• The middle section is more dance-like, quick and with a nimble bow.

• In the final cadence (bars 75-76) I have added a semi-quaver 'cadenza' ('cadence' and 'cadenza' are the same word) just as Fontana would have done. The bass has a single note underneath you, so you have the freedom to play your cadenza any way you want. It should sound like an improvisation, so don't play it rhythmically or mechanically!

Arcangelo Corelli (1653–1713)

23. *Preludio from Sonata No. 10*

Arcangelo Corelli was an Italian composer and violinist, working most of his life in Rome. His Opus 5 Violin Sonatas, from which these movements are drawn, were published on January 1st, 1700, and did indeed mark the beginning of a new era for the violin and its repertoire. Corelli's music was imitated and copied by many composers, both in Italy and abroad, and pupils came from many lands to study with him.

This Preludio from Sonata no. 10 sounds like an aria from a Handel opera (Handel and Corelli did work together for a while).

• Notice that the phrases are quite short, from one to two bars long, although one phrase often joins up with the next one. The character of the music often changes: you need to express these changes in colour and dynamics.

The phrasing in Baroque music must be as clearly defined by the performer as it was by the composer, otherwise the music will sound as confused as a badly read poem:-

Mary had a,
Little lamb it's fleece
Was white as… etc

Giovanni Battista degli Antonii (1636–1698)

24. *Ballo*
25. *Ballo*

Giovanni Battista Degli Antonii was a composer from Bologna, Italy. Like most musicians at the time, he seems to have played several instruments, including the violin and the cornetto. I have put together three movements from his Sonatas to form this mini Dance Suite.

• The first movement has the character of a ceremonial March, perhaps to welcome the arrival of a King or Queen. Play with a full trumpet-like sound; if you like, you could make an echo when a motive is repeated, such as in bar 7 and from the last beat of Bar 8.

• The last one has a French flavour to it: the semiquavers can be swung a little, not played in a rigidly metronomic way. French musicians considered playing such notes equally to be almost vulgar, lacking in sophistication. Listen to the recording and try and imitate it: I've added some little French ornaments as well, which you are welcome to copy!

George Frederic Handel (1685–1759)

26. *Andante* from *Sonata No. 5*

Along with J.S. Bach, Handel is one of the greatest composers of the Baroque era. They were born in the same year, and grew up not far from each other, yet they never met! Handel's parents wanted him to become a lawyer, but music was too strong a passion for him, and he decided to devote his life to it. Whereas Bach worked in courts and churches, wrote only in German and Latin, never travelled very far and never wrote an opera, Handel, who spent some years in Italy before moving to London where he lived for the rest of his life, wrote mostly in Italian and English and wrote nearly 50 operas as well as around 30 Oratorios (written like operas but not staged).

• The rests in bars 2-5 etc should be treated as breaths: breathe in physically at each one, and breathe with your bow-arm also, lifting it slightly above the string and moving towards the frog just enough to be able to continue comfortably.

• In bar 6 the violin part divides into two parts, an upper and a lower one. Play the upper notes more lyrically than the lower ones.

• In bar 7 the long F sharp leads over the bar line, where it clashes (becomes a dissonance) with the bass note G. You should crescendo into the dissonance, making sure you have enough bow left to make the full effect!

• In bars 15-16 the chromatic scale implies a crescendo, so start it quietly.

27. Boure from *Sonata No. 5*

This dance-like movement needs articulation (tiny rests between notes) to make it sound energetic. Stop the bow between the crotchets at the opening, and between the notes in bar 2.

• In bars 5-7 the passage of rising quavers implies a crescendo, so start softly!

• In bar 16 you need to play in second position if we are to reach that top note!

Arcangelo Corelli (1653–1713)

28. Sarabanda from *Sonata No. 7*

The Sarabanda from Corelli's Sonata VII has a haunting air about it. Both halves have the same structure: two 4-bar phrases, the first one divided into two 2-bar phrases.

• The second notes in bars 2, 4, 9 and 11 are the final notes of their phrases, not upbeats to the next phrase.

• This piece displays a typical feature of the sarabande; two strong beats in a bar features frequently in the bass part, for example in bars 1, 5, 6 and 7.

• Bars 13-14 are a hemiola.

• On the recording, you will hear some ornamentation on the repeats: try and copy them or, better still, make up your own!

Michael Farinel (1649-1726)

29. A Division on a Ground

A *Division on a Ground* by French violinist and composer Michel Farinel is a set of divisions (variations) on *La Follia*, a very popular tune from the 16th to the 18th centuries. It was published in London in 1685, the year Bach and Handel were born, in *The Division Violin*, a collection of mostly popular tunes arranged for violin and continuo by John Playford. A 'ground bass' is one that is repeated over and over again, and here the violin part is built over that repeated bass. Composers including Corelli, Vivaldi and Lully also wrote sets of variations on the same theme.

• Each variation has a distinct character, sometimes dance-like, sometimes more lyrical. One thing is sure: the music must always be spirited and interesting and should never sound dull or technical!

Notes sur les pièces et les compositeurs

Three Jacobean Masque Tunes (Trois Airs de masques jacobéens)

1. The Mountebank's Dance at Grayes Inne

2. Adsonns Maske

3. Sir Francis Bacon's Second Masque

Le terme anglais *Jacobean* vient de la forme latine Jacobus du prénom anglais James et renvoie au règne de Jacques VI roi d'Écosse, couronné en 1603 roi d'Angleterre sous le nom de Jacques Ier. Un masque était un divertissement dramatique joué souvent devant des rois et des reines, comprenant musique, danse, chant et texte parlé, interprété par des acteurs en costumes somptueux devant des décors splendides.

• Le premier et le troisième morceau ressemblent à des danses : jouez-les avec un archet vigoureux de façon à ce que votre public ait vraiment envie de danser !

The Mountebank's Masque a été mis en scène en 1618 à la *Gray's Inn* à Londres. *Mountebank* signifie charlatan, escroc.

• La partie rapide doit être jouée deux fois plus vite que l'ouverture plus lente et plus gracieuse.

John Adson (1587–1640) était un compositeur et musicien anglais qui a travaillé principalement dans des théâtres. Son masque, le deuxième morceau, a une qualité lyrique plus prononcée que les deux autres.

Francis Bacon (1561–1626) était un homme très influent aux nombreux talents: philosophe, scientifique, homme d'état et auteur. Cet air composé en son honneur revêt une dignité solennelle bien que la dernière partie ressemble plus à une danse folklorique !

Giulio Caccini (1551–1618)

Trois chansons tirées de *Le nuove musiche*

4. Dalla porta d'oriente

5. Al fonte, al prato

6. Amor, chlattendi

Giulio Caccini était un chanteur et compositeur italien également harpiste et luthiste. Dans son recueil de chansons pour voix seule *Le nuove musiche* (La nouvelle musique, 1602), la partie de chant rendait au mieux le sens des paroles, aidée par l'harmonie de la basse continue. Ceci a marqué un tournant dans l'histoire de la musique, donnant naissance à l'opéra et aux sonates solo.

• Les trois pièces présentées ici sont toutes des chansons. Les virgules symbolisent les respirations que prendrait le chanteur. Vous devez donc aussi respirer aux virgules, à la fois physiquement mais aussi avec votre archet qui doit être légèrement levé au-dessus de la corde. Tous les livres traitant de la musique instrumentale à partir du seizième siècle expliquent l'importance d'imiter les chanteurs : pourquoi donc ne pas trouver des enregistrements de ces chansons et les imiter !

Marco Uccellini (v. 1603–1680)

de la Sinfonie Boscarecia, op. 8

7. Symphonia Septima 'La Gianina'

8. Symphonia Decima Settima 'La Stucgarda'

Marco Uccellini était un compositeur et violoniste italien. Il a travaillé à Modène et devint par la suite maestro di cappella (maître de chapelle) d'une église à Parme. Il a composé des opéras et des ballets, qui ont malheureusement été perdus, ainsi que des sonates (dont certaines montent jusqu'à la sixième position). Ces symphoniae (et non symphonie dans le sens plus tardif et classique du terme) sont des pièces instrumentales, intitulées chacune par le nom de la dame à qui elle est dédiée.

• Écoutez attentivement l'enregistrement et observer les variations de son entre les parties. Une partie en mineur est souvent plus douce qu'une partie en majeur.

Tomaso Cecchino (1583–1644)

9. Sonata Secondo

Venise est une ville exceptionnellement belle de par ses canaux, ses palais splendides et ses magnifiques églises. Autrefois, elle était la capitale de la République de Venise. Tomaso Cecchino a travaillé la plupart de sa vie dans une partie de cet état désormais en Croatie. Comme presque toutes les sonates du XVIIè siècle, cette pièce pouvait être jouée sur tout instrument capable de jouer les notes : une flûte à bec, un *cornetto* (une sortie de trompette en bois) ou un violon.

• Remarquez que la basse, qui ouvre le mouvement, est tout aussi importante que la ligne principale. Si vous avez un ami violoncelliste ou bassoniste, vous pouvez jouer ce morceau en duo. Il est important de marquer les phrasés de façon claire : les indications d'archet que j'ai ajoutées vous aideront.

De 'The Notebook of Anna Magdelaena Bach' (1725)

J.S. Bach (1685–1750)

10. Menuet (BWV Anh. 132)

Jouez ce menuet sur un ton chantant, sans oublier l'élégance et la sérénité qui sont essentielles à une exécution correcte d'un menuet.

• À la mesure 2 et aux autres endroits similaires, laisser votre archet danser légèrement, raccourcissant un peu les notes permettant ainsi au son d'être léger.

De 'The Notebook of Anna Magdelaena Bach' (1725)

Gottfried Heinrich Stölzel (1690–1749)

11. Bist du bei mir (BWV Anh. 119)

Bist du bei mir (Êtes-vous avec moi?) est une magnifique chanson qui a longtemps été attribuée à Bach, mais qui, depuis, est connue pour faire partie d'un opéra de Gottfried Heinrich Stölzel.

• Votre archet est votre voix : il doit chanter ! Plus les mouvements du bras de l'archet seront expressifs, plus le son le sera.

• À la mesure 13, le trille commence par une appogiature marquée qui ne doit pas être trop rapide (comme il s'agit d'un trille du quatrième doigt, ce devrait être facile !)

De 'The Notebook of Anna Magdelaena Bach' (1725)

J.S. Bach (1685–1750)

12. Musette

Une musette est une sorte de cornemuse française. Bien qu'il n'y ait pas de bourdon dans cet instrument, la partie de basse y fait penser car elle répète la même note tel un bourdon.

• Aux mesures 3 et 4, raccourcissez les croches, contrastant ainsi avec le caractère plus chantant des deux premières mesures.

• Les mesures 13 et 14 doivent être jouées doucement et chantant. Les notes des syncopes sont aussi à jouer légère et non lourde.

52

De 'The Notebook of Anna Magdelaena Bach' (1725)
Christian Petzold (1677–1733)

13. Menuet (BWV Anh. 115)

Comme le dixième morceau, ce menuet est en mineur. Il a été composé par l'organiste et compositeur allemand Christian Petzold. Les quatre premières notes doivent être chantées, mais les deux suivantes peuvent être « adoucies » (elles sont moins importantes). Apprendre à distinguer les notes importantes de celles qui le sont moins (appelées « bonnes » et « mauvaises » du temps de Bach) est essentiel pour que la musique reste intéressante.

De 'The Notebook of Anna Magdelaena Bach' (1725)
J.S. Bach (1685–1750)

14. Polonaise (BWV Anh. 119)

Une polonaise est une danse pas trop rapide mais très rythmée, au caractère noble. De nombreux compositeurs baroques l'ont utilisée dans leurs compositions, et elle est restée populaire jusqu'au cours du XIXe siècle.

• Faîtes des coups d'archets brefs et précis. Chaque mesure débute par un accent bien marqué !

William Babell (c.1690–1723)

15. Allegro de la *Sonate VII*

William Babell était un claveciniste, organiste, violoniste et compositeur anglais, qui a probablement étudié avec Handel. L'improvisation était une compétence essentielle d'un musicien baroque, et Babell était particulièrement réputé pour sa capacité à choisir une mélodie et improviser dessus juste après. Certains pensaient même qu'il était meilleur improvisateur qu'Händel lui-même !

• Improviser des nuances était l'un des aspects de cette compétence. À l'époque baroque, les compositeurs inscrivaient rarement les nuances, mais ne pas en jouer rendait la musique sans intérêt. Je n'en ai pas ajouté non plus, donc vous devrez les inventer ! Pour commencer, suivez ce conseil : les notes ascendantes sont à jouer *crescendo* et celles descendantes *diminuendo*. En d'autres termes, les nuances suivent les lignes formées par la musique sur la page. En variant l'intensité des coups d'archets sur chaque note, vous y arriverez facilement.

Jean-Philippe Rameau (1683–1764)

16. La Villageoise

Jean-Philippe Rameau était l'un des plus grands clavecinistes, théoriciens et compositeurs français. Musicien autodidacte, il a écrit de nombreux livres majeurs sur l'harmonie. Il n'a étonnamment composé son premier opéra qu'à 50 ans, puis 20 autres au cours de sa longue vie. La Villageoise est issue de la Suite en mi mineur pour clavecin.

• Comme cette musique s'apparente à une danse, assurez-vous de ne pas la jouer comme une chanson: les notes sont souvent un peu plus courtes que leur valeur. Un bon exemple est la première mesure.

• De plus, notez que toutes les notes de même valeur ne sont pas égales : les deuxièmes notes des mesures 1, 2 et 4 par exemple, sont faibles, comme « résonnant » des premiers temps forts. Les syncopes des mesures 18, 20 et 22 font appel, quant à elles, à un mouvement de l'archet plus marqué mais gracieux. Les tirés que j'ai ajoutés vous aideront à rendre cet effet et à raccourcir les premières notes faibles de ces mesures. Vous apprendrez rapidement à reconnaître les temps forts et faibles et ainsi rendre la musique à la fois élégante et intéressante.

Martino Bitti (1655–1743)

17. Gavotta

Martino Bitti était un violoniste et compositeur italien qui a travaillé principalement à Florence.

• À l'origine, la gavotte était une danse traditionnelle française très populaire au cours de la période baroque. Elle débute sur le dernier temps de la mesure.

• Les mesures 2, 4 et 6 sont fortes et les mesures 1, 3 et 5 faibles. Si vous accentuez le premier temps d'une mesure faible, vous casserez l'équilibre de la musique !

Old English Melody

18. Greensleeves

Greensleeves est une ancienne mélodie anglaise. Mentionnée pour la première fois en 1580 puis citée dans *The Merry Wivevs of Windsor* par Shakespeare, elle est depuis restée populaire. Cette version, certainement différente de celle que vous connaissez, est tirée d'un recueil intitulé *The Division Violin*, publié en 1685 par John Playford, un libraire londonien.

• Chaque phrase de huit mesures est une variation du thème écrite sur une basse répétitive. Certains coups d'archets sont quelque peu ardus, faîtes bien danser l'archet !

• Une fois que vous maîtrisez le morceau, vous pouvez proposer vos propres variations : trouver un ami qui jouera en continu la ligne de basse pendant que vous improviserez... que ça aille ou non ! C'est déjà amusant d'essayer et ne vous découragez pas si vous vous trompez ! Improviser des divisions et des ornements faisait partie de l'apprentissage de tout musicien jusqu'à la fin du XIXe siècle ; et c'est toujours le cas pour les musiciens de jazz et dans la plupart des traditions musicales non occidentales.

Antonio Vivaldi (1678–1741)

19. Adagio de la *Sonate en ré* (RV 798)

Antonio Vivaldi était un violoniste et compositeur italien. Pendant onze ans, il a été *maestro di violino* à l'institution Ospedale della Pietà dans sa Venise natale, enseignant le violon à des jeunes femmes et composant spécialement pour elles. De nos jours, Vivaldi est surtout connu pour ses Quatre Saisons, mais il a également composé 500 concertos, de nombreuses musiques d'église et plusieurs opéras.

• L'adagio (ce terme signifie « à l'aise ») ne doit être joué trop lentement : les croches de la ligne de basse supposent un mouvement constant vers l'avant. Veillez à ne pas accentuer les poussés sur les croches, comme par exemple celles aux mesures 1, 2 et 3 : alléger-les plutôt, compensant ainsi le tempo plus rapide.

• Sur le CD, vous pouvez écouter une version telle qu'elle est écrite et une autre où j'ai ajouté des ornements comme l'aurait probablement fait Vivaldi. Comment je le sais ? Car beaucoup de livres traitant de l'ornementation ont été écrits au cours de la période baroque. Une fois que vous maîtrisez le morceau, vous pouvez vous essayer à jouer les vôtres !

20. Allegro de la *Sonate en ré* (RV 798)

Tout le long de cet Allegro, gardez votre archet vif et léger. N'oubliez pas de varier les nuances en suivant les notes : ascendant donc *crescendo*, descendant donc *diminuendo*.

• Si les notes sont jouées égales, la musique devient très lourde. En réalité, certaines notes sont plus importantes que d'autres. Aux mesures 1 et 2, et aux autres endroits similaires, donnez une bonne impulsion sur la première note et laissez les deux suivantes rebondir dessus, comme si votre archet était une balle rebondissante. La dernière note de chaque mesure est ainsi revitalisée, donnant à la mesure le même rythme que la basse.

• De même la mesure 8 et celles similaires doivent avoir une unique et vive impulsion sur la première note, les quatre suivantes n'étant qu'une réaction passive à cette impulsion. La mesure 23 et celles similaires doivent aussi avoir une unique impulsion sur la première note : ne forcez pas trop avec l'archet sur le reste de la mesure car elle sera trop lourde sinon, comme s'il y avait « trop » de notes.

Henry Purcell (1659–1695)

21. Rondeau tiré de Abdelazar

Henry Purcell est sans doute le plus grand compositeur anglais. Au cours de sa courte vie, il a composé de la musique d'église, pour le théâtre et la Cour, mais aussi de la musique vocale et de chambre. Il est capable de nous transmettre de nombreuses émotions par sa musique parfois exaltante voire amusante mais également quelquefois très triste. Purcell a composé ce morceau pour une mise en scène de 1695 de la pièce *Abdelazar*, soit « la revanche du Maure », de Aphra Behn, l'un des premiers auteurs féminins. Le *Rondo* est devenu connu lorsque Benjamin Britten l'a utilisé comme thème pour son *Young Person's Guide to the Orchestra* (Guide d'orchestre pour les jeunes) quelque 250 ans plus tard.

Un rondeau - Purcell utilisait l'orthographe française - est une composition qui comporte un thème d'ouverture (les huit premières mesures) repris plusieurs fois (aux mesures 9, 17 et 33) entre lesquelles alternent des parties contrastées appelées épisodes.

• Jouez le thème d'un ton enjoué et majestueux avec des coups d'archets nets. Le rythme des mesures 3 à 6 suit la basse avec des accents sur les premières et dernières notes de chaque mesure. L'épisode qui débute à la mesure 25 est la partie la plus calme et la plus lyrique.

La forme de la sonate a été « inventée » en Italie, mais de nombreux compositeurs italiens travaillaient à l'étranger, dans des pays aussi éloignés que l'Angleterre et la Pologne, amenant ainsi les nouveaux styles et techniques baroques.

Giovanni Battista Fontana (1589(?)–1630)

22. Sonata Terza

Giovanni Battista Fontana était un violoniste et compositeur italien dont on ne sait que très peu sur sa vie. Ses six sonates pour violon seul et basse continue font partie d'un recueil de sonates pour un, deux et trois violons publié en 1641. Ces œuvres sont des exemples très probants des débuts de la sonate solo.

L'une des caractéristiques de ces sonates du début du XVII^è siècle est qu'elles n'ont aucun « mouvement » dans le sens actuel du terme mais sont divisées en plusieurs parties contrastées, liées entre elles.

La *Sonata Terza* (Sonate n° 3) comporte beaucoup de parties, mais je ne les ai pas toutes gardées pour que ce soit plus court et plus simple : si vous souhaitez entendre l'œuvre complète, vous pourrez très certainement trouver des enregistrements sur internet, que ce soit au violon ou sur d'autres instruments.

• Nous avons déjà rencontré le rythme de la première mesure: il était très commun dans la musique vénitienne, et fait penser à une fanfare. Pour autant, la première partie peut être jouée de façon plutôt lyrique grâce à un archet souple.

La partie centrale ressemble plus à une danse, l'archet doit donc être rapide et vif.

• Dans la dernière cadence (mesures 75-76), j'ai ajouté une double croche sur la *cadenza* (cadence) tout comme l'aurait fait Fontana. La basse ne joue qu'une note sous votre partie, vous pouvez donc jouer la cadence comme vous le souhaitez, comme si c'était une improvisation. Ne la jouez donc pas de façon rythmique et mécanique !

Arcangelo Corelli (1653–1713)

23. Preludio de la Sonate n° 10

Arcangelo Corelli était un compositeur et violoniste italien, qui a travaillé la majeure partie de sa vie à Rome. Les sonates pour violon opus 5, dont sont tirés ces mouvements, ont été publiées le 1er janvier 1700, et ont marqué un tournant dans l'appréciation de cet instrument et son répertoire. De nombreux compositeurs ont imité et copié la musique de Corelli, en Italie mais aussi à l'étranger, et des élèves de diverses régions venaient travailler avec lui.

Ce prélude de la Sonate n° 10 peut faire penser à une aria d'un opéra de Handel. (Handel et Corelli ont en effet travaillé ensemble un certain temps.)

• Remarquez que les phrases sont relativement courtes, d'une à deux mesures, même si souvent une phrase est liée à la suivante. Le caractère de la musique change régulièrement : vous devez reproduire ces changements de couleur et de nuances.

Dans la musique baroque, le musicien doit reproduire le phrasé tel que le compositeur l'avait pensé, le plus précisément possible, autrement la musique produira le même effet confus qu'un texte mal récité.

Frère Jacques, frère Jacques, Dormez-vous ? Dormez-vous ? Sonnez....

Giovanni Battista degli Antonii (1636–1698)

24. Ballo
25. Ballo

Le compositeur Giovanni Battista Degli Antonii venait de Bologne en Italie. Comme beaucoup de musiciens à l'époque, il savait sûrement jouer de plusieurs instruments, dont le violon et le cornet. J'ai assemblé trois mouvements tirés de ses sonates pour créer cette petite Suite de danses.

• Le premier mouvement ressemble à une marche digne d'une cérémonie, peut-être pour accompagner l'arrivée d'un roi ou d'une reine. Jouez-le avec un son plein comme sur une trompette. Si cela vous plaît, lorsque qu'un motif se répète, vous pouvez le jouer en écho, comme par exemple à la mesure 7 et à partir du dernier temps de la mesure 8.

• La dernière danse a un parfum français. Les doubles croches peuvent être un peu décalées et non jouées en suivant parfaitement le métronome. Les musiciens français trouvaient que jouer de telles notes égales était presque vulgaire, voire manquait de raffinement. Écoutez l'enregistrement et essayer de l'imiter. J'y ai ajouté aussi quelques ornements typiquement français que vous pouvez bien sûr reprendre !

George Frederic Handel (1685–1759)

26. Andante de la *Sonate n° 5*

Tout comme J.-S. Bach, Handel est l'un des plus grands compositeurs de la période baroque. Alors que Bach a travaillé pour des Cours, des églises, n'a écrit qu'en allemand et latin, n'a jamais voyagé loin et ni écrit d'opéra, Handel, qui a vécu quelques années en Italie avant de s'installer à Londres, a écrit majoritairement en italien et en anglais et a composé près de 50 opéras et environ 30 Oratorios.

• Les silences des mesures 2 à 5 etc sont comme des respirations : sur chacun, respirez vraiment mais aussi avec votre bras tenant l'archet, le levant légèrement au-dessus de la corde et l'amenant vers le talon, suffisamment pour retrouver une position confortable et continuer à jouer.

• À la mesure 6, la partie de violon se divise en deux. Jouez les notes de la partie supérieure plus lyriques que celles de la partie inférieure.

• À la mesure 7, le long fa dièse court jusqu'après la barre de mesure, où il vient frotter (devenant une dissonance) avec le sol de la basse. Il faut jouer la dissonance petit à petit en s'assurant qu'il vous reste suffisamment d'archet pour créer l'effet dans son ensemble !

• Aux mesures 15 à 16 la gamme chromatique sous-entend un crescendo, commencez donc doucement.

27. Boure de la *Sonate n° 5*

Ce mouvement s'apparentant à une danse doit être bien articulé (courts silences entre les notes) pour qu'il soit énergique. À l'ouverture, arrêtez l'archet entre les noires et entre les notes à la mesure 2.

• Aux mesures 5 à 7, les croches ascendantes sous-entendent un crescendo, commencez donc doucement.

• À la mesure 16, il faut que vous jouiez en deuxième position pour réussir à atteindre cette note aigüe !

Arcangelo Corelli (1653–1713)

28. Sarabanda de la *Sonate n° 7*

La sarabande de la Sonate n° 7 de Corelli a quelque chose d'envoûtant. Chaque moitié suit la même structure : deux phrases de quatre mesures, la première étant divisée en deux phrases de deux mesures.

• Aux mesures 2, 4, 9 et 11, les deuxièmes notes sont les conclusions de chacune des phrases et non des levées des phrases suivantes.

• Ce morceau comporte une caractéristique typique de la sarabande : dans une mesure, deux temps forts apparaissent souvent dans la partie de basse comme aux mesures 1, 5, 6 et 7 par exemple.

• Les mesures 13 et 14 forment une hémiole.

• Sur le CD, vous entendrez quelques ornements lors des reprises : essayez de les copier ou mieux, d'en inventer !

Michael Farinel (1649–1726)

29. A Division on a Ground

A Division on a Ground du compositeur et violoniste français Michel Farinel est un ensemble de variations sur La Follia, thème très populaire du XVIè au XVIIIè siècles. A Division on a Ground a été publié à Londres en 1685, année de naissance de Bach et Handel, dans le recueil intitulé The Division Violin, regroupant principalement des airs arrangés pour le violon et basse continue par John Playford. Une basse obstinée est une basse qui répète une figure en continu, ici, la partie de violon est construite sur une telle basse. Corelli, Vivaldi et Lully, entre autres, ont composé des variations sur ce même thème.

• Chaque variation a son propre caractère, parfois dansant ou bien plus lyrique. Une chose est sûre : la musique doit toujours être animée et intéressante et ne jamais paraître ennuyeuse ou technique !

Anmerkungen über Stücke und Komponisten

Three Jacobean Masque Tunes (Drei jakobinische Masque-Stücke)

1. The Mountebank's Dance at Grayes Inne

2. Adsonns Maske

3. Sir Francis Bacon's Second Masque

Das Wort *Jacobean* („jakobinisch") stammt von Jacobus, der lateinischen Form des Namens Jakob und bezieht sich auf König Jakob VI von Schottland, der 1603 als Jakob I zum König von England gekrönt wurde.

Eine Masque (Maskenspiel) war eine extravagante Form der höfischen Unterhaltung, die Musik, Tanz, Gesang und Schauspiel vereinte. Dargeboten wurde sie von maskierten Darstellern in prächtigen Kostümen und einem aufwändigen Bühnenbild.

• Das erste und dritte Stück weist jeweils meist Tanzelemente auf und sollte mit kraftvollem Strich gespielt werden, damit das Publikum richtig Lust aufs Tanzen bekommt!

The Mountebank's Masque entstand 1618 im Gray's Inn in London (ein „Mountebank" ist ein Schwindler!)

• Der schnelle Teil sollte doppelt so schnell gespielt werden wie der elegante, langsame Eröffnungsteil.

John Adson (1587–1640) war ein englischer Komponist und Musiker, der hauptsächlich am Theater arbeitete. Seine „Maske" ist gefühlvoller als die beiden anderen.

Francis Bacon (1561–1626) war ein überaus einflussreicher Mann mit vielen Talenten: Philosoph, Wissenschaftler, Staatsmann und Autor. Dieses Stück, das ihm zu Ehren geschrieben wurde, drückt eine vornehme Würde aus, obgleich der letzte Teil eher wie ein Volkstanz klingt!

Giulio Caccini (1551–1618)

Drei Lieder aus *Le nuove musiche*

4. Dalla porta d'oriente

5. Al fonte, al prato

6. Amor, chlattendi

Giulio Caccini war ein italienischer Sänger und Komponist, der auch Harfe und Laute spielte. In seiner Sololiedersammlung mit dem Titel *Le nuove musiche* (*Die neue Musik*, 1602) hatte die Gesangsstimme die Aufgabe, den Sinn des Textes so genau wie möglich wiederzugeben. Unterstützt wurde sie vom Generalbass. Dies verlieh der Musikgeschichte eine völlig neue Richtung, die zur Entstehung der Oper und der Solosonate führte.

• Alle drei Stücke sind Lieder, und wir haben immer dort Atemzeichen in Form von Kommas eingefügt, wo ein Sänger Luft holen würde. Beim Spielen sollte man bei allen Kommas atmen – sowohl körperlich als auch symbolisch durch kurzes Absetzen des Bogens. In jedem Buch über Instrumentalmusik ab dem 16. Jahrhundert steht, dass man die Sänger imitieren muss. Daher sollte man sich auf jeden Fall Aufnahmen dieser Lieder suchen und sie nachspielen!

Marco Uccellini (ca. 1603–1680)

Aus der Sinfonie Boscarecia, op. 8

7. Symphonia Septima „La Gianina'

8. Symphonia Decima Settima „La Stucgarda'

Marco Uccellini war ein italienischer Komponist und Violinist. Er arbeitete in Modena und wurde später „maestro di cappella' (Kapellmeister) an einer Kirche in Parma. Er schrieb Opern und Ballette, die leider alle verschollen sind, sowie zahlreiche Sonaten (von denen einige in der sechsten Lage gespielt werden). Diese „Symphoniae' (keine „Sinfonien' im späteren, klassischen Sinn) sind Instrumentalstücke, die Namen als Titel haben, da jedes Stück einer anderen Dame gewidmet war!

• Höre dir die Aufnahme genau an und achte darauf, wie sich der Klang von einem Teil zum nächsten verändert. Ein Moll-Teil ist oft weicher als ein Dur-Teil.

Tomaso Cecchino (1583–1644)

9. Sonata Secondo

Venedig ist mit seinen Kanälen, prachtvollen Plätzen und Kirchen eine Stadt von einzigartiger Schönheit. Früher war es die Landeshauptstadt der Republik Venedig. Tomaso Cecchino arbeitete fast sein ganzes Leben lang in einem Teil des Landes, der heute Kroatien heißt. Wie die meisten Sonaten aus dem frühen 17. Jahrhundert wäre dieses Stück auf jedem Instrument gespielt worden, mit dem man die Noten spielen konnte: Blockflöte, *cornetto* (eine Art Holztrompete) oder Violine.

• Beachte, dass der Bass, der den Satz eröffnet, genauso wichtig ist wie die Oberstimme. Wenn du einen Freund hast, der Cello oder Fagott spielt, könnt ihr das Stück als Duo spielen. Die Phrasen sollten deutlich zu hören sein; die von mir eingefügten Strichanweisungen helfen dabei.

Aus *Notenbüchlein für Anna Magdalena Bach* (1725)

J.S. Bach (1685–1750)

10. Menuet (BWV Anh. 132)

Dieses Stück sollte singend gespielt werden, wobei immer die Eleganz und Anmut beachtet werden sollte, die für die richtige Ausführung eines Menuetts unerlässlich sind.

• In Takt 2 und an ähnlichen Stellen sollte der Bogen tanzen, d. h. die Noten werden ein wenig kürzer gespielt, was dem Klang eine gewisse Beschwingtheit verleiht.

Aus *Notenbüchlein für Anna Magdalena Bach* (1725)

Gottfried Heinrich Stölzel (1690–1749)

11. Bist du bei mir (BWV Anh. 119)

Bist du bei mir ist ein wunderschönes Lied. Lange dachte man, Bach habe es komponiert, doch jetzt weiß man, dass es aus einer Oper von Gottfried Heinrich Stölzel stammt.

• Der Bogen ist deine Stimme: Er muss singen! Je ausdrucksvoller die Gesten mit dem Bogenarm sind, desto ausdrucksvoller klingt auch das Stück.

• In Takt 13 beginnt der Triller mit einer gefühlvollen Appoggiatura und sollte nicht zu schnell gespielt werden (da er mit dem vierten Finger gespielt wird, sollte das kein Problem sein!)

Aus *Notenbüchlein für Anna Magdalena Bach* (1725)

J.S. Bach (1685–1750)

12. Musette

Eine Musette ist ein Tanz, der nach einem französischen Dudelsack benannt ist. Dieses Stück enthält zwar keinen Bordunton, doch wird ein und dieselbe Note im Bass auf ähnliche Weise wiederholt.

• In Takt 3 und 4 sollten die Achtel kürzer gespielt werden, damit sie einen Kontrast zum eher gesanglichen Charakter der ersten zwei Takte bilden. Takt 13 und 14 sollten sanft und gefühlvoll gespielt werden. Die Synkopen sollten ebenfalls weich und nicht zu schwer sein.

Aus *Notenbüchlein für Anna Magdalena Bach* (1725)
Christian Petzold (1677–1733)
13. Menuet (BWV Anh. 115)

Wie Stück Nr. 10 steht auch dieses Menuett in Moll. Es wurde von dem deutschen Komponisten und Organisten Christian Petzold geschrieben.

Die ersten vier Noten müssen ,gesungen' werden, wohingegen die nächsten beiden ,vernachlässigt' werden können (sie sind nicht so wichtig). Die Unterscheidung zwischen wichtigen und weniger wichtigen Noten (zu Bachs Zeiten wurden sie als ,gute' und ,schlechte' Noten bezeichnet) ist unerlässlich, wenn die Musik nicht langweilig werden soll und gehört daher auf jeden Fall zum Unterrichtsstoff.

Aus *Notenbüchlein für Anna Magdalena Bach* (1725)
J.S. Bach (1685–1750)
14. Polonaise (BWV Anh. 119)

Eine Polonaise ist ein polnischer Tanz, der nicht zu schnell, aber sehr rhythmisch ist und vornehm klingt. Viele Barockkomponisten verwendeten die Polonaise in ihren Kompositionen, und sie erfreute sich bis weit ins 19. Jahrhundert hinein großer Beliebtheit.
• Für dieses Stück sollten kurze, energische Striche verwendet werden. Jeder Takt enthält am Anfang einen ordentlichen Akzent!

William Babell (ca. 1690–1723)
15. Allegro aus der *Sonate VII*

William Babell war ein englischer Cembalist, Organist, Violinist und Komponist, der eventuell von Händel ausgebildet wurde. Improvisation war ein wesentlicher Bestandteil der Ausbildung von Barockmusikern, und Babell war berühmt für sein Talent, eine Melodie zu nehmen und aus dem Stegreif eine eigene Version zu improvisieren. Einige seiner Zeitgenossen waren der Meinung, er könne sogar besser improvisieren als Händel selbst!
• Das Improvisieren mit der Dynamik war ein wesentlicher Aspekt dieser Fähigkeit. Die Barockkomponisten verwendeten nur selten dynamische Zeichen, doch ohne unterschiedliche Lautstärkegrade hätte die Musik furchtbar langweilig geklungen! Ich habe in deiner Stimme keine dynamischen Zeichen hinzugefügt, damit du dir selbst welche ausdenken kannst. Als ersten Schritt kannst du folgende einfache Methode ausprobieren: Aufsteigende Noten werden *crescendo* gespielt und absteigende *diminuendo*. Mit anderen Worten: Die Dynamik folgt der Linie, die man auf der Notenseite sieht. Wenn jede Note mit einer anderen Bogenlänge gespielt wird, ist es kein Problem, diesen Effekt zu erzielen.

Jean-Philippe Rameau (1683–1764)
16. La Villageoise

Jean-Philippe Rameau war einer der berühmtesten Cembalisten, Musiktheoretiker und Komponisten Frankreichs. Er war Autodidakt und schrieb zahlreiche bedeutende Bücher zum Thema Harmonielehre. Seine erste Oper schrieb er erst im Alter von 50 Jahren, gefolgt von weiteren 20 im Laufe seines langen Lebens. La Villageoise (,Die Dorfbewohnerin') stammt aus seiner Suite in

e-Moll für Cembalo. Da diese Musik einige Tanzelemente aufweist, sollte man sie nicht wie ein Lied spielen: Die Noten sollten eher etwas kürzer gespielt werden als ihr theoretischer Wert. Der erste Takt ist ein gutes Beispiel dafür.
• Darüber hinaus sind nicht alle Noten mit demselben Notenwert gleich lang: Die zweite Note in Takt 1, 2 und 4 ist beispielsweise unbetont, wodurch die Eins jeweils stärker betont wird. Die Synkopen in Takt 18, 20 und 22 hingegen erfordern einen stärkeren, aber eleganten Strich. Die Abstriche, die ich eingefügt habe, helfen dabei und verkürzen jeweils die erste, schwächere Note dieser Takte. Du wirst schon bald den Unterschied zwischen betonten und unbetonten Zählzeiten erkennen, der die Musik sowohl elegant als auch abwechslungsreich macht.

Martino Bitti (1655–1743)
17. Gavotta

Martino Bitti war ein italienischer Violinist und Komponist, der hauptsächlich in Florenz arbeitete.
Die Gavotte war ursprünglich ein Volkstanz und in der gesamten Barockzeit beliebt. Sie beginnt auf der letzten Zählzeit des Taktes. Takt 2, 4 und 6 sind stark und Takt 1, 3 und 5 schwach. Betont man die Eins eines schwachen Taktes, wird die Balance der Musik zerstört!

Old English Melody
18. Greensleeves

Greensleeves ist eine alte englische Melodie. Sie wurde zum ersten Mal 1580 in Shakespeares *The Merry Wives of Windsor* erwähnt und erfreut sich seither überaus großer Beliebtheit. Die vorliegende Version, die sich wahrscheinlich von der unterscheidet, die du kennst, stammt aus einer Sammlung mit dem Titel *The Division Violin*, die erstmals 1685 von dem Londoner Buchhändler John Playford herausgegeben wurde.
• Jeder achttaktige Teil stellt eine Variation des Themas dar, das über den Wiederholungen im Bass notiert ist. Einige Striche sind etwas schwierig: Achte darauf, den Bogen tanzen zu lassen!
• Wenn du das Stück beherrschst, kannst du eigene Variationen hinzufügen: Ein Freund kann immer wieder die Bassstimme spielen, während du spielst, was dir gerade in den Sinn kommt… vorausgesetzt, es passt einigermaßen! Es macht bestimmt Spaß, es auszuprobieren. Lass dich nicht abschrecken, wenn du dich verspielst! Das Improvisieren von Variationen und Verzierungen war bis ins 19. Jahrhundert Bestandteil jeder Musikerausbildung und gehört auch heute noch im Jazz und den meisten nicht-westlichen Musiktraditionen dazu.

Antonio Vivaldi (1678–1741)
19. Adagio aus der *Sonate in D-Dur* (RV 798)

Antonio Vivaldi war ein italienischer Violinist und Komponist. Elf Jahre lang arbeitete er in seiner Geburtsstadt Venedig als ,maestro di violino' am Ospedale della Pietà, wo er den jungen Damen Geigenunterricht gab und eigens für sie Werke schrieb. Heute ist Vivaldi vor allem für seine *Vier Jahreszeiten* bekannt, doch schrieb er insgesamt 500 Konzerte, sehr viel Kirchenmusik sowie zahlreiche Opern.
• Das Adagio (das Wort bedeutet ,ruhig') sollte nicht zu langsam gespielt werden: Die Achtel im Bass deuten auf eine konstante Vorwärtsbewegung hin. Achte darauf, die Achtel-Aufstriche nicht zu betonen, z. B. in Takt 1, 2 und 3: Sie sollten leicht gespielt werden, um die Temposteigerung auszugleichen.

• Die CD enthält sowohl die notierte Version als auch eine Version, die ich so verziert habe, wie Vivaldi es vermutlich getan hätte. Woher ich das weiß? Weil in der Barockzeit viele Bücher zum Thema Verzierungen geschrieben wurden. Wenn du das Stück erst einmal gut kennst, kannst du eigene Verzierungen ausprobieren.

20. *Allegro* aus der *Sonate in D-Dur* (RV 798)

Das Allegro sollte durchgängig mit lebhaftem, leichtem Strich gespielt werden. Achte darauf, die Lautstärke zu variieren, indem du der Kontur der Noten folgst: nach oben bedeutet crescendo und nach unten *diminuendo*.

• Wenn Noten zu gleichförmig gespielt werden, wirkt die Musik oft sehr schwer. Tatsache ist, dass einige Noten wichtiger sind als andere! In Takt 1 und 2 und an ähnlichen Stellen sollte die erste Note betont werden, und die beiden nächsten sollten passiv von ihr abprallen, als ob der Bogen ein aufprallender Ball wäre. Die letzte Note im Takt erhält dann neue Energie, was dem Takt denselben Rhythmus verleiht wie dem Bass.

• Genauso sollte die erste Note in Takt 8 und an ähnlichen Stellen einen einzigen, aktiven Impuls erhalten, während die folgenden vier Noten passiv auf diesen Impuls reagieren. In Takt 23 und an ähnlichen Stellen sollte ebenfalls die erste Note betont werden: Der Bogen sollte im restlichen Takt nicht zu stark aufgesetzt werden, da der Klang sonst zu schwer wird, als ob ,zu viele' Noten da wären.

Henry Purcell (1659–1695)

21. *Rondeau* aus *Abdelazar*

Henry Purcell ist wohl der berühmteste englische Komponist. In seinem sehr kurzen Leben komponierte er Musik für die Kirche, das Theater und den Hof sowie zahlreiche Vokal- und Kammermusikstücke. Bemerkenswert ist seine große Bandbreite an Gefühlen, die er vermittelt, indem er seine Musik teils fröhlich oder sogar lustig und teils fast unerträglich traurig gestaltet. Purcell schrieb dieses Stück 1695 für eine Produktion des Theaterstücks *Abdelazar* oder *Die Rache der Mauren* von Aphra Behn, die eine der ersten Schriftstellerinnen war. Das *Rondo* wurde berühmt, als Benjamin Britten es etwa 250 Jahre später als Thema für seinen *Young Person's Guide to the Orchestra* verwendete.

Ein Rondo (Purcell verwendet die französische Schreibweise ,Rondeau') ist eine Komposition, bei der ein Anfangsthema (die ersten acht Takte) mehrere Male wiederkehrt (in Takt 9, 17 und 33). Die kontrastierenden Teile dazwischen werden als ,Couplets' bezeichnet.

• Das Thema sollte majestätisch und mit forschen Bogenstrichen gespielt werden. Der Rhythmus in Takt 3-6 folgt dem Bass, wobei jeweils die erste und letzte Note im Takt betont werden. Das Couplet, das in Takt 25 beginnt, ist der gefühlvollste Teil.

Die Sonate wurde zwar in Italien ,erfunden', doch arbeiteten viele italienische Komponisten im Ausland – häufig in so entfernten Ländern wie England und Polen – und nahmen die neuen Stilmittel und Techniken des Barock mit dorthin.

Giovanni Battista Fontana (1589(?)–1630)

22. *Sonata Terza*

Giovanni Battista Fontana war ein italienischer Violinist und Komponist, über dessen Leben sehr wenig bekannt ist. Seine sechs Sonaten für Solovioline und Basso continuo sind Teil einer Sonatensammlung für eine, zwei und drei Violinen, die 1641 veröffentlicht wurde. Die Werke gehören zu den bedeutendsten

Beispielen der frühen Solosonate.

Ein Merkmal dieser Sonaten aus dem frühen 17. Jahrhundert ist, dass sie keine ,Sätze' im späteren Sinne hatten, sondern aus vielen kontrastierenden und miteinander verbundenen Teilen bestanden. Die *Sonata Terza* (Sonate Nr. 3) besteht aus vielen Teilen, von denen ich einige weggelassen habe, um das Stück zu verkürzen und zu vereinfachen: Wenn du dir das ganze Werk anhören möchtest, findest du im Internet sicherlich Aufnahmen, die mit einer Violine oder anderen Instrumenten eingespielt wurden.

• Den Rhythmus im Anfangstakt haben wir schon einmal gesehen: Er kommt häufig in der venezianischen Musik vor und erinnert an eine Fanfare. Meist kann der erste Teil jedoch gefühlvoll und singend gespielt werden. Der Mittelteil ist eher wie ein Tanz – schnell und mit lebhaftem Strich.

• In der letzten Kadenz (Takt 75-76) habe ich im Sinne Fontanas eine Sechzehntel-Kadenz eingefügt. Der Bass spielt nur eine einzige Note unter deiner Stimme, so dass du deine Kadenz beliebig gestalten kannst. Sie sollte wie eine Improvisation klingen und daher nicht rhythmisch oder mechanisch gespielt werden!

Arcangelo Corelli (1653–1713)

23. *Preludio* aus der *Sonate Nr. 10*

Arcangelo Corelli war ein italienischer Komponist und Violinist, der hauptsächlich in Rom tätig war. Seine Violinsonaten Opus 5, aus denen diese Sätze hier stammen, wurden am 1. Januar 1700 veröffentlicht und markierten den Beginn einer neuen Ära für die Violine und ihre Spielliteratur. Corellis Musik wurde sowohl in Italien als auch im Ausland von vielen Komponisten kopiert, und Schüler kamen aus zahlreichen Ländern, um von ihm ausgebildet zu werden.

Dieses Preludio aus der Sonate Nr. 10 klingt wie eine Arie aus einer Händel-Oper (Händel und Corelli arbeiteten tatsächlich eine Zeitlang zusammen).

• Beachte, dass die Phrasen recht kurz sind (ein bis zwei Takte lang), wobei eine Phrase oft in die nächste übergeht. Die musikalische Stimmung ändert sich häufig: Diese Veränderungen sollten durch die Tonfarbe und Lautstärke ausgedrückt werden.

Die Phrasierung in der Barockmusik muss vom Interpreten genauso festgelegt werden wie vom Komponisten. Andernfalls klingt die Musik so wirr wie ein schlecht vorgetragenes Gedicht:

Das ist der,
Daumen, der schüttelt
die, Pflaumen der hebt
sie auf der, trägt…etc.

Giovanni Battista degli Antonii (1636-1698)

24. *Ballo*
25. *Ballo*

Giovanni Battista Degli Antonii war ein Komponist aus der italienischen Stadt Bologna. Wie die meisten Musiker seiner Zeit spielte er anscheinend mehrere Instrumente, u. a. Violine und *cornetto*. Ich habe drei Sätze aus seinen Sonaten zu dieser Mini-Tanzsuite zusammengestellt.

• Der erste Satz gleicht einem Festmarsch, vielleicht zur Ankunft eines Königs oder einer Königin. Er sollte mit einem vollen, trompetenhaften Klang gespielt werden. Wenn du willst, kannst du bei der Wiederholung eines Motivs ein Echo spielen, z. B. in Takt 7

58

oder ab der letzten Zählzeit von Takt 8.

• Der letzte Satz klingt ein wenig französisch: Die Sechzehntel können swingend gespielt werden, also nicht streng metronomisch. Für französische Musiker grenzte es an Geschmacklosigkeit, solche Noten gleichmäßig zu spielen – war dies doch ein Zeichen fehlender Raffinesse. Höre dir die Aufnahme an und versuche, sie nachzuspielen: Ich habe auch ein paar kleine französische Verzierungen eingefügt, die du ebenfalls gerne nachspielen kannst!

Georg Friedrich Händel (1685–1759)
26. *Andante* aus der *Sonate Nr. 5*

Zusammen mit J.S. Bach ist Händel einer der bedeutendsten Komponisten der Barockzeit. Während Bach an Höfen und in Kirchen arbeitete, nur in deutscher und lateinischer Sprache schrieb, nie weit reiste und keine Oper schrieb, komponierte Händel, der einige Jahre in Italien lebte, bevor er nach London ging, meist auf Italienisch und Englisch und schrieb fast 50 Opern und ca. 30 Oratorien.

• Die Pausen in Takt 2-5 sollten wie Atemzeichen behandelt werden: In jeder Pause sollte sowohl körperlich als auch symbolisch mit dem Bogenarm eingeatmet werden, indem dieser etwas über die Saite Richtung Frosch angehoben wird – gerade so viel, dass du bequem weiterspielen kannst.

• In Takt 6 teilt sich die Violinstimme in zwei Stimmen auf, eine Ober- und eine Unterstimme. Spiele die hohen Noten gefühlvoller als die tiefen.

• In Takt 7 wird das lange Fis über den Taktstrich hinweg gespielt, wo es mit dem Basston G kollidiert (d. h. eine Dissonanz bildet). Spiele ein *Crescendo* in diese Dissonanz hinein und achte darauf, dass du genug Bogen hast, um den Effekt voll zur Geltung zu bringen!

• In Takt 15-16 enthält die chromatische Tonleiter ein *Crescendo*; du solltest also leise anfangen.

27. *Bourée* aus der *Sonate Nr. 5*

Dieser Tanz erfordert eine gute Artikulation (winzige Pausen zwischen den Noten), damit er schwungvoll klingt. Der Bogen sollte zwischen den Vierteln am Anfang und den Noten in Takt 2 abgesetzt werden.

In Takt 5-7 enthält die aufsteigende Achtelpassage ein *Crescendo*; du solltest also leise anfangen.

In Takt 16 musst du in der zweiten Lage spielen, um den hohen Ton zu bekommen!

Arcangelo Corelli (1653–1713)
28. *Sarabanda* aus der *Sonate Nr. 7*

Die Sarabande aus Corellis Sonate VII hat etwas Eindringliches. Beide Teile haben denselben Aufbau: zwei viertaktige Phrasen, von denen die erste in zwei zweitaktige Phrasen unterteilt ist.

• Die zweite Note in Takt 2, 4, 9 und 11 ist jeweils die letzte Note der Phrase, also kein Auftakt zur nächsten Phrase.

• Dieses Stück enthält ein typisches Merkmal der Sarabande: Der Bass enthält häufig zwei betonte Schläge pro Takt, z. B. in Takt 1, 5, 6 und 7.

• Die Takte 13-14 bilden eine Hemiole.

• Die Aufnahme enthält einige Verzierungen bei den Wiederholungen: Versuche sie nachzuspielen, oder am besten denkst du dir selbst welche aus!

Michael Farinel (1649–1726)
29. *A Division on a Ground*

A Division on a Ground von dem französischen Violinisten und Komponisten Michel Farinel besteht aus einem Satz Variationen über *La Follia*, ein sehr beliebtes Stück aus dem 16.-18. Jahrhundert. Es wurde 1685, im Geburtsjahr von Bach und Händel, in London in *The Division Violin* von John Playford veröffentlicht, einer Sammlung bekannter Stücke, die für Violine und Basso continuo bearbeitet waren. Ein Generalbass ist eine Bassstimme, die ständig wiederholt wird. Hier baut sich die Violinstimme über den Wiederholungen im Bass auf. Komponisten wie Corelli, Vivaldi und Lully schrieben ebenfalls Variationen über dieses Thema.

• Jede Variation hat ihren eigenen Charakter, manchmal tänzerisch, manchmal gefühlvoll. Eines steht jedoch fest: Die Musik muss immer mit Begeisterung gespielt werden und abwechslungsreich sein und sollte nie langweilig oder technisch klingen!

Walter Reiter

Walter Reiter is internationally recognised as a leading Baroque violinist, teacher, leader and conductor. He is Professor of Baroque Violin in the Royal Conservatory of The Hague and at Trinity Laban Conservatoire of Music in London, and gives courses as far afield as Israel and Cuba. He has led and directed Baroque Orchestras all over the world, and his critically acclaimed solo CDs include Sonatas by Mondonville (awarded the 'Choc' label by the French magazine Diapason), Vivaldi's Violin Sonatas Op.2 and the Biber Mystery Sonatas. For many years a devoted teacher of young children, he is uniquely placed to combine these two interests in this anthology.

www.walterreiter.co.uk

Walter Reiter est reconnu internationalement comme un violoniste, enseignant et chef d'orchestre baroque éminent. Il enseigne le violon baroque au Conservatoire royal de La Haye, au Trinity Laban Conservatoire de musique de Londres, et donne également des cours en Israël et à Cuba. Il conduit et dirige des orchestres baroques dans le monde entier, et ses enregistrements en tant que soliste, encensés par les critiques, comportent entre autres des Sonates de Mondonville (qui ont reçu le label « Choc » attribué par le magazine Diapason), les Sonates pour violon Op.2 de Vivaldi et les Sonates du Mystère de Biber. Professeur dévoué depuis des années à ses jeunes élèves et passionné par la musique baroque, il est donc tout particulièrement bien placé pour réaliser cette anthologie.

www.walterreiter.co.uk

Walter Reiter ist ein international anerkannter führender Barockviolinist, Lehrer, künstlerischer Leiter und Dirigent. Er ist Professor für Barockvioline am Königlichen Konservatorium in Den Haag und am Trinity Laban Conservatoire of Music in London und lehrt auch in weiter entfernten Ländern wie Israel und Kuba. Er hat Barockorchester aus der ganzen Welt geleitet und dirigiert, und seine von der Kritik gefeierten Solo-CDs enthalten u.a. Sonaten von Mondonville (mit dem ‚Choc' der französischen Zeitschrift Diapason ausgezeichnet), Vivaldis Violinsonaten op. 2 und die Mystery Sonatas von Biber. Da Reiter außerdem seit Jahren Kinder unterrichtet, ist es ihm gelungen, diese beiden Interessen in dieser Anthologie hervorragend miteinander zu verbinden.

www.walterreiter.co.uk

CD/MP3 Track List / Plages du CD/MP3 / CD/MP3-Titelverzeichnis

This CD contains 29 audio tracks of full versions of the pieces that can be played on a normal CD player. There are also 29 MP3 files of play-along tracks stored in a separate folder on the CD which can be listened to on a computer or MP3 player.

Ce CD contient 29 pistes audio correspondent aux enregistrements complets des morceaux et pouvant être lus sur un lecteur CD normal. Il contient également 29 pistes d'accompagnement dans un fichier séparé, à écouter sur un ordinateur ou un lecteur MP3.

Auf dieser CD sind 29 audio tracks einer Vollversion der Stücke, die auf einem normalen CD-player abgespielt werden können. In einem separaten Ordner auf der CD befinden sich 29 MP3 files einer Mitspiel-Version (play-along), die auf einem Computer oder einem MP 3-Player abspielbar sind.

No.	Title	Composer	Duration
	Three Jacobean Masque Tunes		
1.	The Mountebank's Dance at Grayes Inne	Anonymous	2:11
2.	Adsonns Maske	John Adson	1:21
3.	Sir Francis Bacon's Second Masque	Anonymous	1:01
	Three songs from 'Le nuove musiche'		
4.	Dalla porta d'oriente	Giulio Caccini	0:47
5.	Al fonte, al prato	Giulio Caccini	1:21
6.	Amor, ch'attendi	Giulio Caccini	0:39
	From Sinfonie Boscarecia, op. 8		
7.	Symphonia Septima 'La Gianina'	Marco Uccellini	2:17
8.	Symphonia Decima Settima 'La Stucgarda'	Marco Uccellini	1:17
9.	Sonata Seconda	Tomaso Cecchino	0:51
	From The Notebook of Anna Magdalena Bach (1725)		
10.	Menuet (BWV Anh. 132)	Johann Sebastian Bach	0:49
11.	Bist du bei mir (BWV 508)	Gottfried Heinrich Stölzel	2:17
12.	Musette	Johann Sebastian Bach	0:58
13.	Menuet (BWV Anh. 115)	Christian Petzold	1:39
14.	Polonaise (BWV Anh. 119)	Johann Sebastian Bach	1:03
15.	Allegro from *Sonata VII*	William Babell	1:21
16.	La Villageoise	Jean-Philippe Rameau	1:07
17.	Gavotta	Martino Bitti	1:08
18.	Greensleeves	Old English Melody	4:03
19.	Adagio from *Sonata in D* (RV 798)	Antonio Vivaldi	1:35
20.	Allegro from *Sonata in D* (RV 798)	Antonio Vivaldi	1:34
21.	Rondeau from Abdelazar	Henry Purcell	1:33
22.	Sonata Terza	Giovanni Battista Fontana	2:27
23.	Preludio from *Sonata No. 10*	Arcangelo Corelli	1:49
24.	Ballo	Giovanni Battista degli Antonii	1:40
25.	Ballo	Giovanni Battista degli Antonii	1:01
26.	Andante from *Sonata No. 5*	George Frederic Handel	1:44
27.	Boure from *Sonata No. 5*	George Frederic Handel	1:00
28.	Sarabanda from *Sonata No. 7*	Arcangelo Corelli	1:42
29.	A Division on a Ground	Michael Farinel	3:57
30.	Tuning Notes		0:27

Total Duration: 46:49